I'm the Chef!

Crabtree Publishing Company

PMB 16A, 350 Fifth Avenue
Suite 3308, New York, NY
10118

612 Welland Avenue,
St. Catharines, Ontario
Canada L2M 5V6

Created by **McRae Books**

Coordinating Editor: Ellen Rodger
Project Editor: John Crossingham
Production Coordinator: Rosie Gowsell
Production Assistance: Mary-Anne Luzba
Consulting Chef: Dan Fudge

McRae Books Srl.
Project Manager: Anne McRae
Editors: Alison Wilson
Photography: Marco Lanza, Walter Mericchi
Set Design: Rosalba Gioffrè
Design: Marco Nardi
Layout and cutouts: Adriano Nardi, Laura Ottina, Giovanni Mattioli
Special thanks to: Mastrociliegia (Fiesole), Eugenio Taccini (Montelupo Fiorentino), Maioliche Otello Dolfi (Camaioni Montelupo) for their assistance during the production of this book.
Color separations: Fotolito Toscana, Florence, Italy

CATALOGING-IN-PUBLICATION DATA

Lee, Frances, 1971-
    The young chef's Chinese cookbook / Frances Lee.
      p. cm. -- (I'm the chef)
    Includes index.
    ISBN 0-7787-0280-4 (RLB) -- ISBN 0-7787-0294-4 (pbk.)
    1. Cookery, Chinese--Juvenile literature. 2. Quick and easy cookery--Juvenile literature. [1. Cookery, Chinese.] I. Title. II. Series.
    TX724.C5L428 2001
    641.5951--dc21

2001017292
LC

123456789
Printed and bound in Italy by Nuova GEP, Cremona
987654321

I'm the Chef!

The Young Chef's
CHINESE
COOKBOOK

Crabtree
www.crabtreebooks.com

List of Contents

DISCLAIMER

The recipes in this book are suitable for children aged 9 and up. They have been prepared in our test kitchen by a mother of three young children and are all safe for children of that age. Since cooking involves the use of knives, boiling water, and other potentially dangerous equipment and procedures, we strongly recommend that adults supervise children at all times while they prepare the recipes in this book. The publishers and copyright owners will not accept any responsibility for accidents that may occur as children prepare these dishes.

Introduction

China is one of the world's oldest civilizations, and its **cuisine** is famous around the world. This cookbook teaches you how to make Chinese dishes such as spring rolls, dim sum, fried rice, and many others. Step-by-step photographs and text help to explain all 15 recipes. This book also examines one of the most important Chinese festivals — Chinese New Year. Food is a large part of this festival. You can learn to prepare a dish that the Chinese serve to celebrate the beginning of the new year.

Spring rolls

Spring rolls are a favorite **appetizer**, and they are not too difficult to make at home. They can be made ahead of time and kept in the refrigerator until you are ready to cook them. You may change the filling to suit your own tastes.

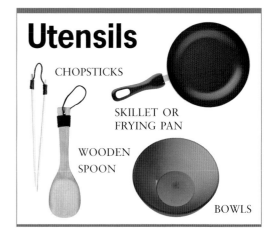

Utensils

CHOPSTICKS

SKILLET OR FRYING PAN

WOODEN SPOON

BOWLS

1 Place a large frying pan on the stove over high heat. Add 2 tablespoons (30 ml) of the oil. Stir fry the turnip or cabbage and carrots until they are lightly cooked.

2 Add the water chestnuts and bamboo shoots to the pan and stir until they are heated.

3 Add the shrimp, sugar, soy sauce, salt and pepper to the pan and mix well. Pour the ingredients into a large bowl and leave to cool.

TIPS & TRICKS

Spring rolls must be fried in hot oil to be crispy. If the oil is not hot enough the rolls will be soggy. If it is too hot, the rolls will burn. To test if the oil is hot enough, take a bit of bread and put it in the oil. If the bread sizzles and browns, the oil is hot enough. Boiling oil can splatter and cause nasty burns. Never use it to fry anything unless an adult helps you.

5 Prepare the spring roll skins for filling as explained on the package. Place 2 tablespoons (30 ml) of the mixture in the center of each skin. Take two opposite ends of the skin and fold one over the other, using the egg like glue to seal the edges. Wet the other two ends with the egg and roll into a log shape. Repeat until all the mixture is used.

4 Crack open the egg and **beat** it in a small bowl using chopsticks or a fork.

6 Heat the remaining oil in a deep pan until very hot. Slip the spring rolls into the oil and fry until golden brown, turning frequently so that they brown evenly all over.

7 Using a slotted spoon, remove the cooked rolls from the pan and place on paper towels to absorb the extra oil. Serve hot.

Ingredients

4 cups (1 liter) vegetable oil

1 cup (250 ml) shredded turnip or green cabbage

1 cup (250 ml) shredded carrot

4 tablespoons (60 ml) **diced** water chestnuts, canned or fresh

1 small can shredded bamboo shoots

½ cup (125 ml) diced shrimp, cooked

dash of sugar

2 tablespoons (30 ml) soy sauce

1 egg

salt and pepper to taste

1 package of small spring roll skins

Shrimp and pork dim sum

These little dumplings are a classic dim sum dish. In **Cantonese** cuisine, dim sum is usually served at brunch. A dim sum meal consists of a variety of steamed and deep-fried items, such as dumplings and mini spring rolls, and ends with custard tarts.

Utensils

GRATER

STEAMER

WOODEN
SPOON

LARGE BOWL

LARGE POT OR **WOK**

1 Combine all the ingredients, except the **wonton** skins, in a large bowl and mix until it is smooth and without lumps.

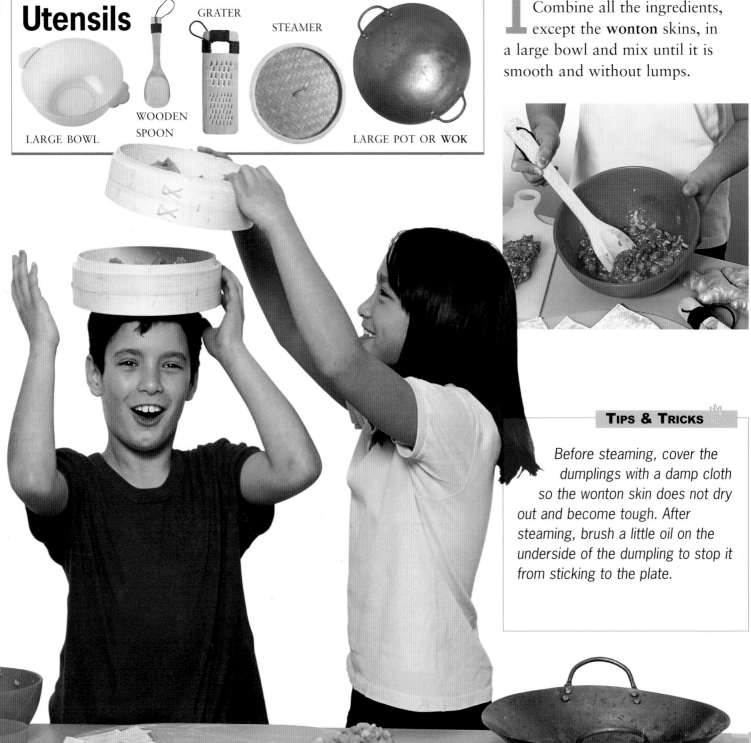

TIPS & TRICKS

Before steaming, cover the dumplings with a damp cloth so the wonton skin does not dry out and become tough. After steaming, brush a little oil on the underside of the dumpling to stop it from sticking to the plate.

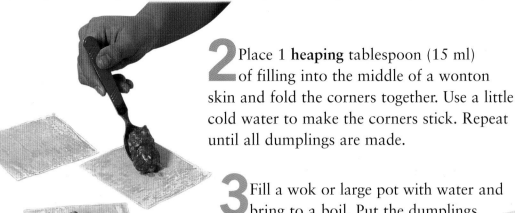

2 Place 1 **heaping** tablespoon (15 ml) of filling into the middle of a wonton skin and fold the corners together. Use a little cold water to make the corners stick. Repeat until all dumplings are made.

3 Fill a wok or large pot with water and bring to a boil. Put the dumplings in the steamer and place it over the pot of boiling water. Cover the steamer with the lid.

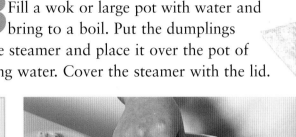

4 Steam for about 20 minutes or until the meat is cooked through. Serve the dim sum warm with some light soy sauce and sliced ginger or chili sauce.

Ingredients

1 tablespoon (15 ml) grated ginger

2 cups (1 lb/450 g) finely **minced** pork

1 cup (250 ml) **chopped** shelled shrimp

1 tablespoon (15 ml) light soy sauce

½ tablespoon (8 ml) sesame oil

½ tablespoon (8 ml) sugar

1 egg

1 tablespoon (15 ml) cornstarch

½ teaspoon (3 ml) white pepper

1 package wonton skins, thawed

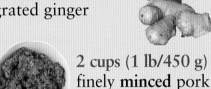

Sweetcorn soup with crabmeat

Cold drinks and other beverages are not normally served at a Chinese family meal. Instead, people usually serve a bowl of soup. Soups have a long tradition in Chinese cuisine. In fact, a Chinese poem written over 2,200 years ago talks about a person eating a "sour and bitter soup."

Ingredients

 6 cups (1.5 liters) chicken stock (made with hot water and a chicken stock cube)

 1 cup (250 ml) fresh corn kernels

8 oz (250 g) cooked real or artificial crabmeat

3–4 slices fresh ginger

1 egg white

 1 teaspoon (5 ml) sesame oil

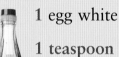 1 tablespoon (15 ml) light soy sauce

dash of salt

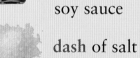 2 teaspoons (10 ml) cornstarch

dash of white pepper

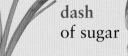 dash of sugar

2 green onions, chopped

1 tablespoon (15 ml) cold water

1 Place the chicken stock in a large pot and bring it to a boil. Add the corn and sliced ginger and **simmer** over low heat for about 15 minutes until the corn is cooked.

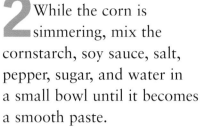

2 While the corn is simmering, mix the cornstarch, soy sauce, salt, pepper, sugar, and water in a small bowl until it becomes a smooth paste.

3 Once the corn is cooked, pour the soy sauce paste into the soup. Turn the heat up to medium and stir until the soup starts to boil.

4 Use a spoon to add the crabmeat to the soup. Stir gently so that you do not get splashed with the boiling soup. Simmer for 5 more minutes.

6 Use a slotted spoon to remove the slices of ginger from the soup. Sprinkle soup with green onions and extra pepper. Serve hot.

5 In another bowl, beat the egg white and the sesame oil together. Now slowly add this mixture into the soup. As you pour the mixture into the pot, stir with a fork or a pair of chopsticks. The egg white should become thin and stringy.

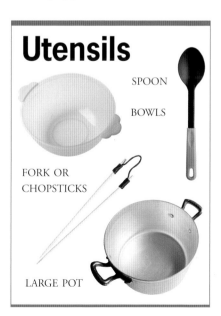

Utensils

SPOON

BOWLS

FORK OR
CHOPSTICKS

LARGE POT

Four-color soup

This vegetable dish can be made even more healthy by adding 8 oz (250 g) of egg noodles to the soup. In Chinese homes, a large bowl of this soup is often placed at the center of the table. Each person has a flat-bottomed soup spoon to dip into the bowl during the meal.

Utensils

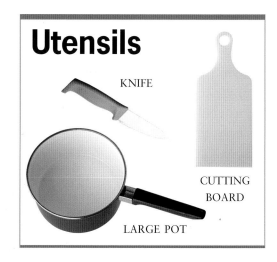

KNIFE

CUTTING BOARD

LARGE POT

1 Cut the tomatoes, mushrooms, and carrots into bite-sized cubes. Hold the handle of the knife firmly in one hand and use the other hand to hold the vegetables. Keep your fingers well away from the blade at all times.

2 Place the chicken stock and the carrots in a large pot. Bring the stock to a boil over medium heat. Simmer for about 5 minutes.

3 Add the spinach, mushrooms, and tomatoes. Stir carefully until the soup returns to a boil.

4 Add the soy sauce, salt, and sugar. Simmer for 1–2 minutes, then serve.

Ingredients

6 cups (1.5 liters) chicken stock (made with boiling water and a stock cube)

2 fresh tomatoes

10 button mushrooms

2 small carrots

7 oz (200 g) fresh spinach leaves

2 teaspoons (10 ml) light soy sauce

dash of sugar

dash of salt

Sweet and sour prawns

Chinese cuisine can be divided into four major regions. Most of the early Chinese **immigrants** to the West came from the Canton region. North Americans are familiar with Cantonese Chinese food. The sweet and sour sauce in this recipe is a Cantonese sauce. It is also delicious with pork or chicken instead of the prawns.

1 Place the prawns in a bowl with 2 tablespoons (30 ml) of the soy sauce. **Marinate** for 30 minutes.

2 Beat the egg in a small bowl. Using chopsticks or your fingers dip the prawns into the egg.

3 Place 3 tablespoons (45 ml) of the cornstarch on a plate. **Dredge** the prawns in the cornstarch.

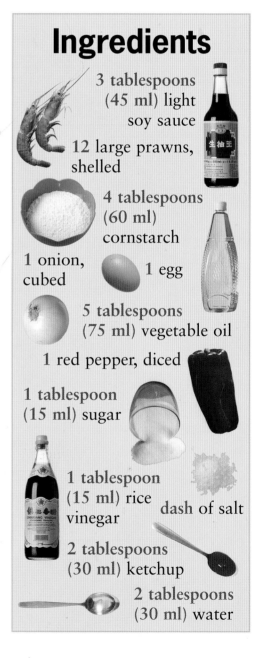

Ingredients

- 3 tablespoons (45 ml) light soy sauce
- 12 large prawns, shelled
- 4 tablespoons (60 ml) cornstarch
- 1 onion, cubed
- 1 egg
- 5 tablespoons (75 ml) vegetable oil
- 1 red pepper, diced
- 1 tablespoon (15 ml) sugar
- 1 tablespoon (15 ml) rice vinegar
- dash of salt
- 2 tablespoons (30 ml) ketchup
- 2 tablespoons (30 ml) water

5 Stir fry the onion and red pepper for 2–3 minutes.

TIPS & TRICKS

You can adjust the sauce by adding more or less sugar and vinegar. More sugar makes the sauce sweeter, while more vinegar makes it more sour. If you do not have rice vinegar, use half a tablespoon (8 ml) of lemon juice instead. If you use pork or chicken, cut the meat into cubes and prepare in the same way as the prawns.

4 Heat the oil in the wok. Add the prawns and cook until they turn an orangy-pink. Be careful not to get splattered by the oil—have an adult help you. Use a slotted spoon to remove the prawns. Place them on paper towels. Pour out most of the oil, except 1 tablespoon (15 ml).

17

Utensils

BOWLS

CHOPSTICKS

WOK OR LARGE FRYING PAN

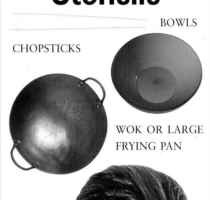

6 Place the cooked prawns back in the wok and mix well.

7 In a bowl, mix the remaining soy sauce, remaining cornstarch, salt, sugar, rice vinegar, ketchup, and water. Then add these ingredients to the wok and stir until the sauce is thick. Serve hot. You may top this dish with sliced oranges or spring onions.

Tofu with pork

Tofu, also called bean curd, has a slightly nutty taste that blends in well with strong flavors. Tofu is made from soy milk and is very healthy. It is a common high **protein** food in many parts of Asia where less meat is eaten than in North America or Europe. You can find tofu in Asian supermarkets and health food stores.

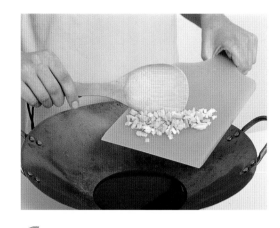

1 Place the oil, garlic, and ginger in a wok on medium high. **Sauté** for 2 minutes. Now add the other ingredients except the pork, tofu, and onions and bring them to a boil.

2 When the sauce is bubbling, add the pork and cook for about 10 minutes, stirring continuously.

TIPS & TRICKS

The sauce that is made in step 1 can be prepared ahead of time and stored in the refrigerator until you need it. If you do not like pork, use chicken or beef instead.

Utensils

WOK OR FRYING PAN

WOODEN SPOON

KNIFE

CUTTING BOARD

3 Cut the tofu into bite-sized pieces and slice the green onions coarsely. Take care to hold the knife firmly by the handle with one hand and hold the tofu and onions with your other hand. Keep your fingers well away from the blade at all times.

4 Add the tofu to the wok and stir carefully.

5 Sprinkle with the green onions, and toss very carefully using chopsticks or a spoon. Serve hot.

Ingredients

1 clove garlic, minced

1 teaspoon (5 ml) ginger, minced

2 teaspoons (10 ml) light soy sauce

2 teaspoons (10 ml) dark soy sauce

1 teaspoon (5 ml) sesame oil

1 teaspoon (5 ml) sugar

dash of salt

1 teaspoon (5 ml) cornstarch

dash of white pepper

4 tablespoons (60 ml) water

1 cup (½ lb/250 g) ground pork

1 lb (500 g) soft tofu

2 green onions

Braised mushrooms

Chinese dried mushrooms can be found in Asian food stores and in many supermarkets. They come in plastic packages and need to be soaked in hot water before they are cooked. In this recipe, they are simmered in a sauce over low heat for 30 to 40 minutes. This cooking technique is called "**braising**."

20

1 Soak the mushrooms in 2 cups (500 ml) of hot water for about 20 minutes. They should be soft.

Ingredients

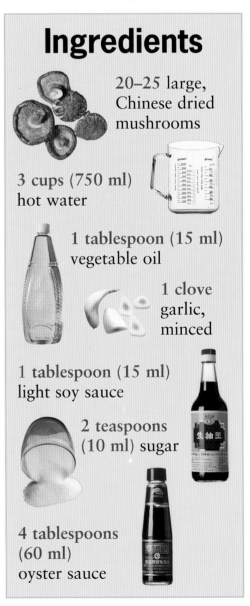

20–25 large, Chinese dried mushrooms

3 cups (750 ml) hot water

1 tablespoon (15 ml) vegetable oil

1 clove garlic, minced

1 tablespoon (15 ml) light soy sauce

2 teaspoons (10 ml) sugar

4 tablespoons (60 ml) oyster sauce

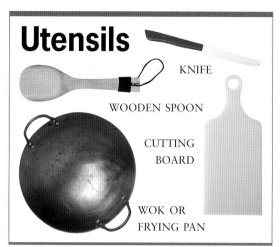

Utensils

KNIFE

WOODEN SPOON

CUTTING BOARD

WOK OR FRYING PAN

2 Drain the mushrooms and dry them with a cloth. Use a table knife to cut off the stems.

3 Heat the oil in the wok and sauté the garlic over medium heat until it is soft.

4 Add the soy sauce, oyster sauce, sugar, 1 cup (250 ml) hot water, and the mushrooms to the wok. Heat until the mixture is bubbling.

TIPS & TRICKS

If you can find them, replace some of the dried mushrooms with fresh shitake mushrooms. Their different texture will give the dish an even better taste. Do not use button mushrooms in this dish. If the mushrooms are fresh, skip step 1. For added flavor, use chicken stock instead of water in the sauce.

5 Turn the heat down and partially cover the wok with a lid. Simmer until most of the liquid has **evaporated**. Serve hot.

Chinese New Year

The Chinese calendar is based on **lunar** and **solar** movements—the days and months are marked by the movements of the sun and moon. Chinese New Year falls on a different day each year, because it is the day of the first new moon of the new year. Chinese New Year is probably the biggest and most important celebration in Chinese culture, and it is celebrated by Chinese all over the world. Colors, food, and symbols all play a big role in making sure the New Year is full of good fortune. The festival lasts 15 days and begins on New Year's Eve. On this evening, family members gather for a large dinner. New Year's Eve and New Year's Day are important to the family. Even if children have moved far away, they will try to come home for Chinese New Year. That is why the New Year's Eve dinner is also called the Reunion Dinner.

Children receive "hongbaos" at Chinese New Year, red envelopes filled with money and decorated with lucky symbols.

New Year's Cake

- 5 cups (1250 ml) glutinous rice flour
- 1⅔ cups (415 ml) brown sugar
- 1⅔ cups (415 ml) boiling water

Sift the flour (buy this special sticky flour at an Asian food store) into a large mixing bowl. Put the sugar in the boiling water and stir until it dissolves. Pour the water and sugar into the flour and mix well. Line an 8-inch Chinese steaming basket with parchment paper. Pour the mixture into the basket and level the top. Place the steaming basket over a pot of boiling water and steam for 2 hours. To test if the cake is cooked, insert a chopstick into the center. If it comes out dry, the cake is ready. Invert the cooked cake and remove the paper. When cool, wrap in foil and refrigerate for 2 days before cutting into four- or six-sided shapes.

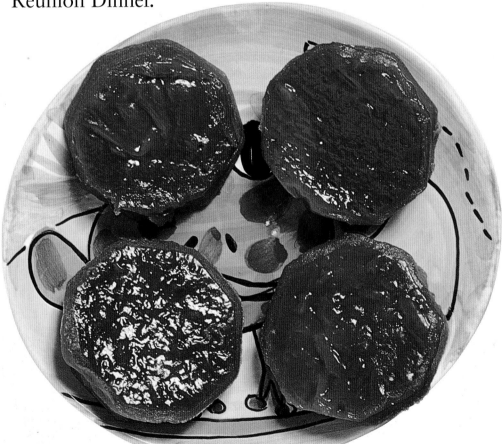

There are many traditional foods that are eaten during Chinese New Year. A large amount of food is prepared to show that the family will have good fortune in the coming year. All the dishes have special meanings. For example, chicken stands for prosperity and fish represents togetherness and abundance. Desserts are also popular and represent a happy life. One favorite dessert is "tang yuan" a dumpling made of **glutinous rice** flour rolled into balls and stuffed with a sweet filling of peanuts or sesame. This is commonly eaten on the last day of the Chinese New Year.

A New Year Legend

Most people agree that the Chinese word "*Nian*," which means year, was the name of a monster that ate people on New Year's Eve. The people were frightened of Nian but an old man came to their rescue. He told Nian, "I have heard of your ferocious power, but can you swallow the beasts of prey on earth instead of helpless humans?" The monster agreed and stopped eating people. The old man told people to put up red paper decorations on their windows and doors at each year's end. The color red would scare away Nian. Even today, the Chinese hang red paper decorations during new year.

Orange is the color of good luck. On Chinese New Year, bring two mandarin oranges for your host. You will also receive two oranges when you leave.

Vegetables with oyster sauce

Lightly boiled or steamed vegetables are a common part of Chinese cuisine. Make sure that these vegetables are crisp and not overcooked. They will taste better and are better for you. Overcooked vegetables can lose some of their vitamins.

TIPS & TRICKS

For a sauce with more flavor, slice a green onion thinly and sauté it in 1 tablespoon (15 ml) of vegetable oil and sesame oil. Drizzle the vegetables with the oil and onions.

1 Fill a large pot half full with cold water and a dash of salt. Place it over high heat and boil.

2 When the water is boiling, add the vegetables. Do not cook them too long. The vegetables should still be crisp and have a good crunch to them.

4 Arrange the vegetables nicely on a serving dish. Pour the oyster sauce over the top and serve hot. Try topping them with sesame seeds as well.

3 Take the vegetables out using a pair of chopsticks or tongs. Shake off the extra water.

Utensils

LARGE POT

CHOPSTICKS
OR TONGS

Ingredients

dash of salt

6 to 8 stalks green leafy vegetable, such as kailan or choi sim

2 tablespoons (30 ml) oyster sauce

Chinese omelet

Traditionally, eggs are not served as a main dish in Chinese cooking. This style of omelet, however, has become popular. It is quick and easy to prepare, and can be served at breakfast, lunch, or dinner. Try adding your own favorite foods to this omelet.

Utensils

CHOPSTICKS

BOWL

SPATULA

SKILLET OR
FRYING PAN

1 Combine the onion, meat, soy sauce, and salt in a mixing bowl. Mix until it is smooth and without large lumps.

2 Beat the eggs in a separate bowl until they are light and frothy. Add the egg to the meat and onion mixture.

Ingredients

1 small white onion, chopped

1 cup (¼ lb/125 g) diced ham
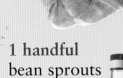

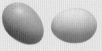
1 handful bean sprouts

½ tablespoon (8 ml) light soy sauce

2 eggs

1 teaspoon (5 ml) salt

2 green onions, chopped

2 tablespoons (30 ml) vegetable oil

For the sauce

½ cup (125 ml) chicken stock

2 teaspoons (10 ml) thick soy sauce

dash of sugar

2 teaspoons (10 ml) cornstarch

3 Heat the oil in a frying pan and slowly pour in all of the egg mixture. When the omelet gets a little puffy and the underside is golden brown, add the bean sprouts and spring onions. Flip the omelet over and cook until the other side is brown too.

TIPS & TRICKS

Try using crabmeat or diced roast pork instead of the ham in this recipe. When cooking the omelet, let the sides set and then push them toward the center of the pan. Tip the pan and let the excess egg mixture flow to the sides. Your omelet will cook more evenly and it will be easier to turn over. Also shake the pan while cooking to make the omelet fluffier.

4 As the omelet is cooking, mix all the ingredients for the sauce together in a saucepan and bring to a boil. Pour the sauce over the omelet or serve separately.

27

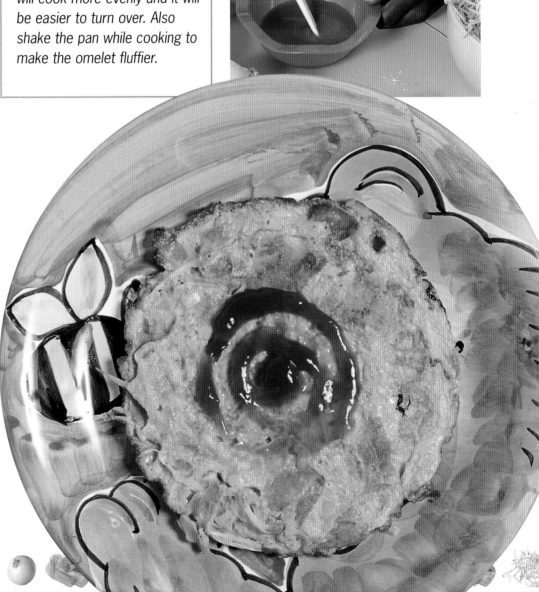

Fried rice

This dish is very popular at Chinese restaurants. Usually fried rice is served in Chinese homes as a one-dish meal, although it is also used instead of steamed rice to go with a meal. At special banquets, fried rice is served toward the end of the meal to fill up anyone who did not get enough to eat!

28

Ingredients

1 cup
(½ lb/250 g)
chopped ham
or cooked
shrimp

1 egg

1 cup (250 ml)
fresh or
thawed frozen
vegetables (corn,
peas, and carrots)

4 cups
(1000 ml)
cooked long
grain rice

2 cloves
garlic, finely
chopped

1 tablespoon
(15 ml) light
soy sauce

2 tablespoons (30 ml)
vegetable oil

1 Add 1 tablespoon (15 ml) of the oil to the wok then place over medium heat.

2 Add the garlic and stir fry until it turns pale golden brown. Be careful not to burn the garlic because it will make the dish taste bitter.

3 Add the ham or shrimp, together with the vegetables to the wok. Stir fry for 1 minute.

4 Add the rice and stir fry until all the ingredients are well mixed. Place the rice mixture on a plate. Add the remaining oil to the wok.

29

5 Beat the egg in a bowl, then add it to the wok. Stir with a fork or chopsticks to scramble the egg. When cooked, put the rice mixture back into the wok. Pour the soy sauce on top and stir fry until well mixed. Serve hot.

TIPS & TRICKS

Fried rice should not be sticky— the grains should be separate and "dry." To get dry rice, use rice left over from the day before. If you do not have any rice from last night's dinner, make sure that the rice you use is cooked and left to cool before you start preparing your fried rice.

Long-life noodles

Noodles are popular in Chinese cuisine. They are always served at birthday parties, because the long strands are believed to be symbols of long life. To have a long life, people try to eat the noodles whole, without biting through the strands. Eating noodles whole takes quite a bit of practice, so make this dish often!

2 Heat the oil in a wok. When it is hot, stir fry the minced ginger and garlic until golden brown.

Utensils

WOK OR LARGE FRYING PAN

CHOPSTICKS OR TONGS

KNIFE

WOODEN SPOON

CHOPPING BOARD

1 If using dried noodles, follow the instructions on the package to cook them. Drain and set aside.

3 Add the pork and stir fry until it is well cooked and pale gold.

TIPS & TRICKS

To avoid having the noodles stick together before cooking, toss them in a little oil. Then lay them on a plate until you need them. Stir the noodles with care after adding them to the wok to avoid breaking them. If you cannot find fish cake in an Asian supermarket, use cooked shrimp instead. If you cannot find fresh bean sprouts, thinly sliced Chinese cabbage works well. Both vegetables give a crunch to the dish and balance out the soft noodles.

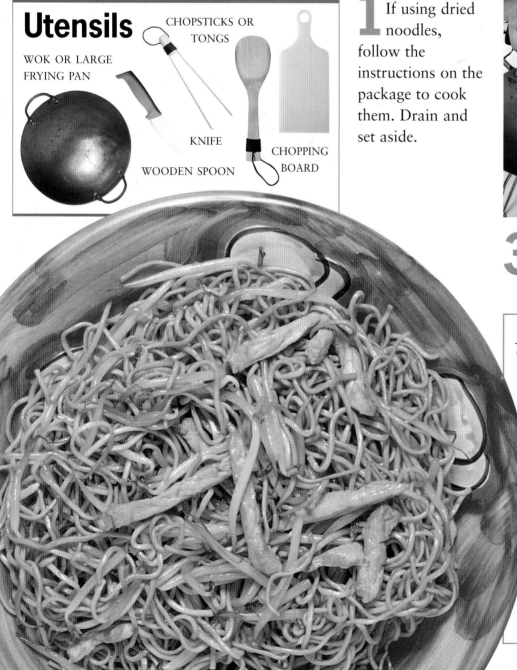

Ingredients

8 oz (250 g) fresh
or dried egg noodles

2 tablespoons
(30 ml) vegetable oil

1 teaspoon (5 ml)
ginger, minced

2–3 cloves
garlic, minced

3½ oz (100 g)
sliced pork

3½ oz (100 g)
bean sprouts

3½ oz (100 g)
sliced fish cake

1 tablespoon
(15 ml) light
soy sauce

1 tablespoon
(15 ml)
oyster sauce

5 Add the noodles to the wok and stir fry another 2 to 3 minutes.

4 Add the bean sprouts and fish cake and stir fry for 2 to 3 minutes more.

6 Pour in the soy sauce and oyster sauce, and stir fry until all ingredients are well mixed. Serve hot.

Chicken porridge

This porridge will warm you up on cold winter evenings, although it takes a while to cook. Keep an eye on the pot to make sure it does not burn or boil over. Try adding to the dish–use small amounts of garlic, ginger, or lemon juice.

1 Simmer the chicken breasts in a pot of boiling water for about 15 minutes. Remove the breasts, and save the water in the pot. This water is now chicken stock.

2 Rinse the rice under cold running water. Place 4 cups (1 liter) of the chicken stock in a pot and add the rice and ginger. Bring the pot to a boil, then lower the heat. Simmer without a lid for about 1½ hours, or until rice is very soft. Keep the heat low so that the porridge does not boil over and stir often so it does not stick. If the porridge becomes too thick to stir, add more chicken stock to the pot.

3 While the porridge is cooking, chop the cooked chicken breasts and place to one side.

TIPS & TRICKS

For a different flavor, replace the chicken with the same quantity of sliced fish or prawns. Also try using half long grain rice and half glutinous rice, so that the porridge is thicker and creamier. Some Chinese grocery stores also sell something called "broken rice." This rice cooks more quickly and it is perfect for porridge.

Ingredients

2 chicken breasts, boneless and skinless

1 cup (250 ml) long grain rice

4 slices ginger

salt to taste

few drops of sesame oil

few drops of light soy sauce

1 tablespoon (15 ml) chopped coriander

2 green onions, chopped

Utensils

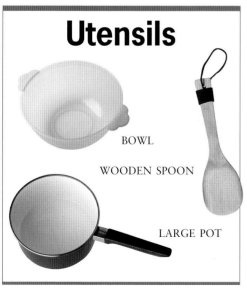

BOWL

WOODEN SPOON

LARGE POT

4 When it is ready, the porridge should be thick and creamy.

5 Place the porridge in a serving bowl. Drizzle it with sesame oil and soy sauce and stir. Top with chicken and add salt. **Garnish** with coriander and green onion.

Red bean soup

In Chinese cuisine sweet soups are often served as a dessert at the end of the meal. While red bean soup is not common in Chinese restaurants, it is one of the most popular desserts in Chinese homes. Best of all, this sweet soup is easy to make!

TIPS & TRICKS

To add more flavor to this dish, try adding some shredded orange **zest** to the soup as it is cooking.

1 Soak the beans in a large bowl of cold water overnight.

2 The next day, boil a large pot of water. Drain the beans and add them to the boiling water.

3 Cook the beans for about 1½ hours until they are soft. If you like firmer beans, cook them for a shorter time.

4 Stir in the sugar and cook for 5 to 10 minutes more. Serve the soup hot.

Ingredients

5 cups (1¼ liters) cold water

1 cup (250 ml) dried red beans

about ½ cup (125 ml) sugar

Utensils

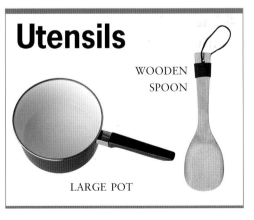

WOODEN SPOON

LARGE POT

Egg custard tarts

Egg custard tarts are the perfect way to finish a Chinese meal. The egg custard tarts can be made with either flaky or short pastry, although the traditional tart is made with a flaky pastry. Choose the pastry you think tastes better.

Ingredients

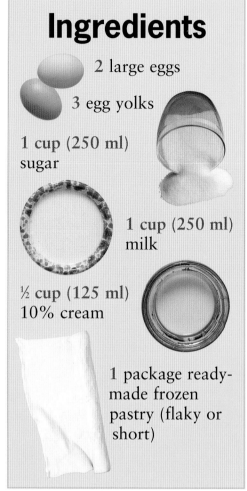

2 large eggs

3 egg yolks

1 cup (250 ml) sugar

1 cup (250 ml) milk

½ cup (125 ml) 10% cream

1 package ready-made frozen pastry (flaky or short)

1 Preheat the oven to 300°F (150°C).

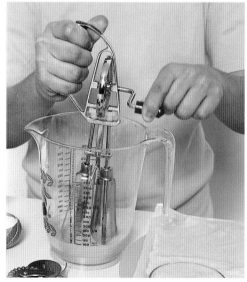

2 Combine the egg yolks and whole eggs in a jug or bowl. Beat them slowly with the egg beater.

Utensils

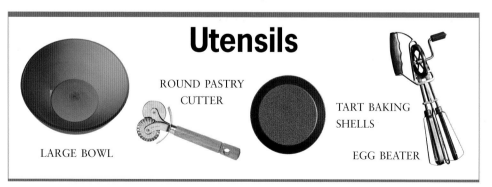

LARGE BOWL

ROUND PASTRY CUTTER

TART BAKING SHELLS

EGG BEATER

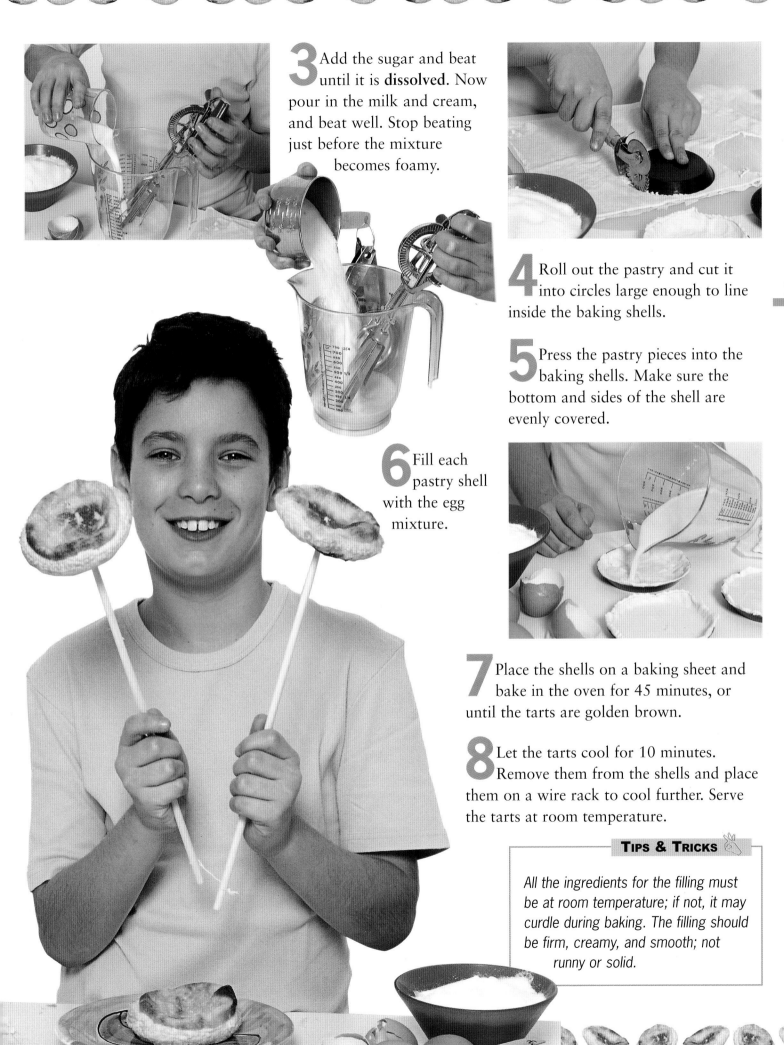

3 Add the sugar and beat until it is **dissolved**. Now pour in the milk and cream, and beat well. Stop beating just before the mixture becomes foamy.

4 Roll out the pastry and cut it into circles large enough to line inside the baking shells.

5 Press the pastry pieces into the baking shells. Make sure the bottom and sides of the shell are evenly covered.

6 Fill each pastry shell with the egg mixture.

7 Place the shells on a baking sheet and bake in the oven for 45 minutes, or until the tarts are golden brown.

8 Let the tarts cool for 10 minutes. Remove them from the shells and place them on a wire rack to cool further. Serve the tarts at room temperature.

TIPS & TRICKS

All the ingredients for the filling must be at room temperature; if not, it may curdle during baking. The filling should be firm, creamy, and smooth; not runny or solid.

Glossary

appetizer A small dish served before the main course

beat To mix a liquid or soft paste rapidly

Bok Choy A green leafy Chinese vegetable

braise To simmer food slowly in a sauce

Cantonese Describing something native to the Canton region of southern China

coriander A herb used in cooking; also known as *cilantro*

cuisine A style of cooking

dice To cut food into tiny cubes using a knife

dissolve When something, such as sugar, disappears into a liquid, such as water

dredge To cover a food item in a substance such as flour or starch

evaporate When a liquid, such as water, is heated until it turns into vapor or gas

garnish To add a portion of food to the side of a main dish as decoration

glutinous rice Rice that is sticky and thick when it is cooked

heaping Describing a measurement that is slightly larger than normal

immigrant A person who has left his or her native country to live in a new one

lunar Describing something that relates to the moon

marinate To soak a food item in a sauce for a long time to give the food extra flavor

mince To cut or chop into very small pieces

protein A natural substance found in foods such as meat and beans. It is needed by all living things

sauté To quickly fry food in a small amount of oil

simmer To cook just at or below a liquid's boiling point

solar Describing something that relates to the sun

thawed To change from a frozen solid to a liquid by warming

tofu A protein-rich food made from an extract of soybeans, used in salads and cooked foods

wonton A small dumpling made of a thin rice noodle sheet wrapped around food

zest Shredded peel of citrus fruits, such as oranges or lemons, that is used to flavor foods

Index